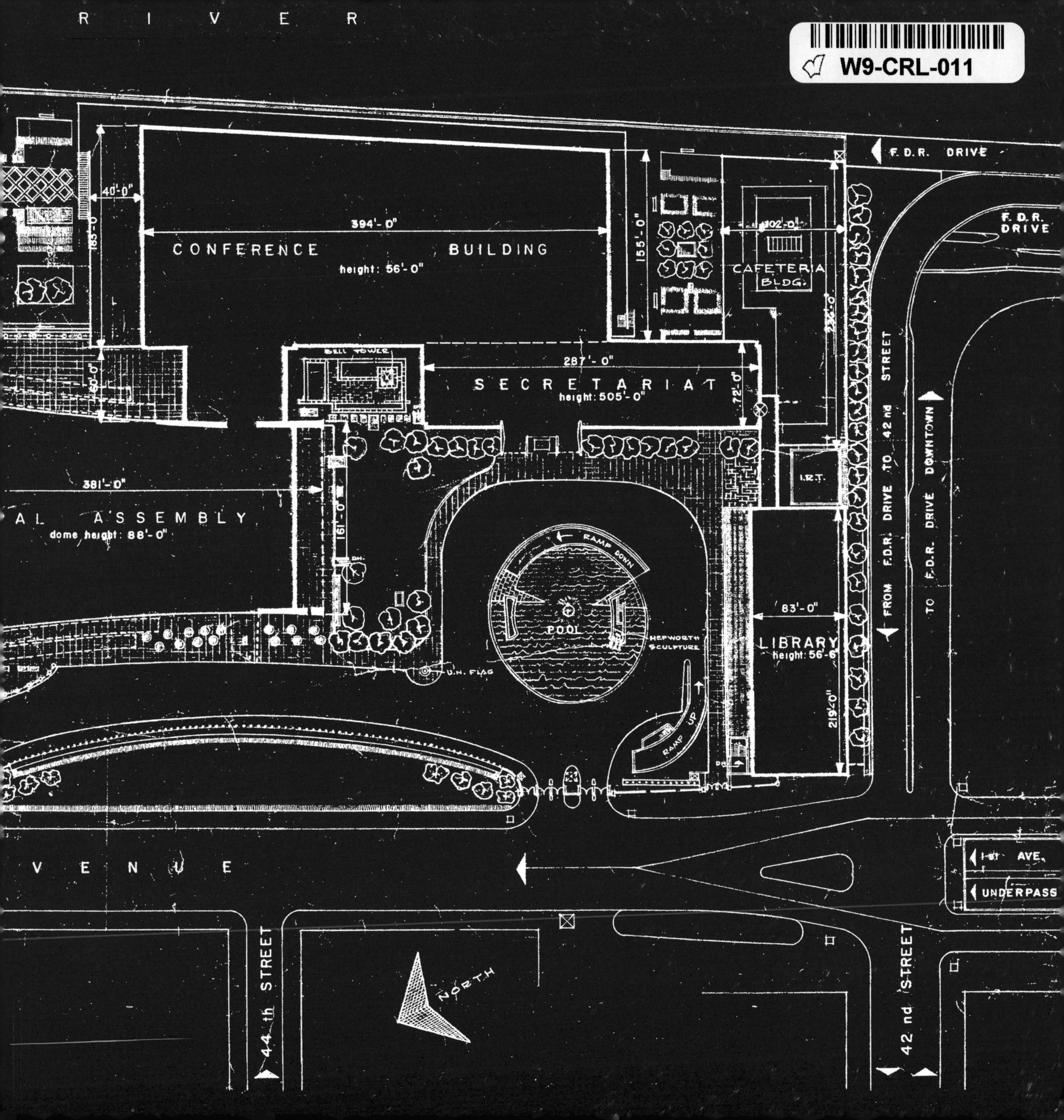

RIVER

40'-0"

185'-0"

394'-0"

CONFERENCE BUILDING
height: 56'-0"

155'-0"

F.D.R. DRIVE

F.D.R. DRIVE

102'-0"

CAFETERIA BLDG.

60'-0"

BELL TOWER

287'-0"

72'-0"

SECRETARIAT
height: 505'-0"

226'-0"

FROM F.D.R. DRIVE TO 42nd STREET

TO F.D.R. DRIVE DOWNTOWN

381'-0"

AL ASSEMBLY
dome height: 88'-0"

161'-0"

I.R.T.

RAMP DOWN

POOL

HEPWORTH SCULPTURE

83'-0"

LIBRARY
height: 56'-6"

219'-0"

U.N. FLAG

RAMP UP

1st AVE.

UNDERPASS

VENUE

44th STREET

NORTH

42nd STREET

INTERNATIONAL TERRITORY

INTERNATIONAL TERRITORY

The United Nations 1945–95

───◆───

ADAM BARTOS

AND

CHRISTOPHER HITCHENS

VERSO

London · New York

First published by Verso 1994

© Text Christopher Hitchens

© Photographs Adam Bartos

Verso

UK: 6 Meard Street, London W1V 3HR

USA: 29 West 35th Street, New York, NY 10001–2291

Verso is the imprint of New Left Books

ISBN 1–85984–901–6

British Library Cataloguing in Publication Data

A catalogue record for this book is available from the British Library

Library of Congress Cataloging-in-Publication Data

A catalogue record for this book is available from the Library of Congress

Typeset by York House Typographic Ltd, London

Printed and bound in the UK by

B.A.S. Printers Limited

Of the truths that remain hidden though useful, knowledge of temporal world governance is most useful and most unknown. Since this knowledge is not directly gainful, it has been neglected by all.

DANTE ALIGHIERI (*De Monarchia*)

CONTENTS

ACKNOWLEDGEMENTS

In preparing this short essay, I was the beneficiary of two pieces of extreme courtesy and generosity. Mr George A. Dudley, FAIA, let me see the advance proofs of his book *A Workshop for Peace: Designing the United Nations Headquarters*, which had for some time been in preparation by the Architectural History Foundation and the MIT Press. This record by a close participant of the evolution of the design of the United Nations will come to stand as the exhaustive aesthetic and historical account. To Mr Dudley and to his publisher, Mrs Victoria Newhouse, I am truly and immensely grateful.

Sir Brian Urquhart and Mr Erskine Childers are known around the terrestrial globe for their lifelong commitment to the ideals of the UN Charter. That they should have shown me their work-in-progress, *Renewing the United Nations System*, was typical of the generosity of spirit which they have both demonstrated throughout long and arduous careers.

I am very grateful to Dr Colin MacCabe of the British Film Institute for suggesting the meeting between myself and Adam Bartos.

CHRISTOPHER HITCHENS
Washington DC, May 1994

INTRODUCTION

In the spring of 1994 I was walking down the promenade which skirts the edge of Roosevelt Island – Manhattan's Other Island – and gives such a commanding view of the East River and the Big City. My companion was Erskine Childers, a long-time Irish diplomat, author, United Nations civil servant and namesake grandson of the brave Republican who was executed on the instigation of Winston Churchill for his opposition to the Treaty of 1921 by which Ireland was partitioned. He was pointing out some of the local topography; the southern end of Roosevelt Island is built on landfill furnished by rubble from the London blitz, said rubble being transported as ballast in the holds of convoy ships during the Battle of the Atlantic. And there hove into view the down-river perspective of the United Nations headquarters building, a distinctive white and glass oblong which most New Yorkers have ceased to notice as they battle the traffic up and down FDR Drive. 'There', said Childers, 'is the office of the first universal social contract.'

Though I knew that another ancestor, Thomas Baron Erskine, had been Lord Chancellor of England and had defended Tom Paine's subversive *Rights of Man*, I had never quite thought of it in that light before. For many politically engaged citizens, I suspect, the United Nations exists in a parallel universe of bureaucracy and diplomacy; a world of suits

1

and briefcases and portfolios, where pious resolutions mock by their wording the unsmiling compromises that triumph in the end. The concept of 'contract' seemed present enough, as in 'high contracting parties' and in the seals and emblems of high-level agreement. But of the universal and the ideal there remained scant evidence. In my youth there had been rather worthy clubs at school dedicated to the promulgation of the United Nations Charter. (Ours, I remember, had been resonantly entitled the Council for Education in World Citizenship, and had allowed co-educational membership as an added inducement.) But this was only politics in the sense of good works and 'meaningful negotiations', and for those of us who did become convinced internationalists there seemed to be more urgent and pressing claims. The UN was where things got fudged and where the most banal statesmen of one's immediate acquaintance could take an annual opportunity to sound Utopian. It was dominated by the nuclear club and by the superpowers. It was an arena for paperwork and hypocrisy.

As I took the cable car back to Manhattan, however, I called on my memory. The UN stage had seen some remarkable plays enacted upon it: the early decision to create the state of Israel, and the later decision to welcome the chairman of the Palestine Liberation Organization (otherwise excluded from the United States) to the podium as President of a landless people; the decision, in the absence of the Soviet delegate, to go to war as a world body in Korea; the setting in which British and French colonialism, thwarted by the American vote, effectively folded its Middle Eastern tent in 1956; the nominal authority during the 'peace' effort in the Congo, during which Patrice Lumumba lost his life to murderers and the first serious Secretary-General, Dag Hammarskjöld, lost his also; the cockpit for the Cuba crisis with Adlai Stevenson, darling of American liberals, lying his way through a justification of the Bay of Pigs. Later, the scene of a face-saving form of words which allowed the nuclear master to stay their hand. Berlin. Formosa. U Thant's noble but impotent protests at the promiscuous aerial destruction of Vietnam. Khrushchev pounding the table with his shoe, the stony faces of the delegation behind him giving a clue (according to insiders) to the imminence of his deposition by the party *apparat*. Archbishop Makarios came to this podium in 1974, as Haile Selassie had once come to the League of Nations, to plead for an invaded country which he no longer ruled.

Warrants for the prosecution of war had been issued by the General Assembly in the cases of the Falklands/Malvinas Islands and the driving of Iraq from Kuwait. On a kinder, gentler note, declarations of human rights and emancipation had been promulgated from the same address, securing at the least a nominal acceptance by governments who could – sometimes – be surprised to be confronted by their own signatures. And for an organization set up exclusively by declared belligerents in the struggle against Nazi imperialism and its allies, there had been the awkward disclosure of the past of Kurt Waldheim.

I thought of the United Nations personnel I had met in the course of my work. The French-Canadian soldiers who had guided me along the no-man's-land in Nicosia, where the armies of two NATO countries faced each other along a slum-strip of ruin and futility. Then the Irish soldiers in southern Lebanon, cheerfully helping a small and defenceless country whose vital signs were ebbing away. In contrast, the grim border of Korea at Panmunjom, where the Greek and Turkish flags actually flew side by side as members of the 'United Nations' forces, and a terrific concentration of nuclear and conventional forces stretched away on either side of a frozen landscape. The exiguous-looking blue-and-white flags on either side of the Golan Heights. My friend Berndt Carlsson, the dedicated Swedish socialist who advised the Secretary-General on Namibia and was murdered in the explosion of Pan Am flight 103 before he could witness the long-overdue independence that he had done so much to bring about. Jose-Maria Mendeluce, the brilliant young Basque who – having exerted himself to the limit in Kurdistan on behalf of the UN High Commision for Refugees – was transferred to Bosnia and tried to alert an indifferent world to the realities of 'ethnic cleansing'. The Nigerian and Jordanian regulars, mustered out of Africa and the Middle East and given a taste of European tribalism on the Croatian frontier. Bored-looking Swedes and baffled Americans, stationed in Skopje Macedonia or FYROM to defend an acronym from annexation by any one of three neighbours.

On the day I was talking to Erskine Childers, the United Nations 'peacekeepers' in Bosnia and in Rwanda were reduced to a self-denying role in which their only authority and ability consisted in acting to defend themselves. In other parts of the globe the situation was perhaps not quite so farcically governed by the Weberian principle that officialdom's objective is its own preservation. (If Prussia could be defined as an army that had a state, the UN was looking very much like an aggregation of states without an army.) But still, in Cyprus and Korea and the Near East, the United Nations dugouts and patrols had often become part of the geometry of the stalemate. On the other hand, in that same week Nelson Mandela's party was racing to victory in South Africa's first elections, and Mr Mandela had been effectively recognized as the leader of a disenfranchised people by the institutions of the UN long before he could vote or even speak in his own cause.

'Don't forget', Childers had told me, 'that the architects of that place' – pointing down-river again – 'were told to calculate for a maximum of seventy members.' In 1947, the General Assembly boasted fifty-five member states and the subsequent arrivals were imagined to be chiefly European. Today the figure for membership is one hundred and sixty-six (although there may be some further and belated European additions to that total). Thus the *structure* of the institution, in all senses, and likewise its *architecture*, in all declensions, struck me as an intriguing place to begin. (The meditative unpeopled photographs of Adam Bartos were my other inspiration here. There is something eloquent in their address to the relationship between structure and function, and also in their register of the work and passage of time.)

I

ARCHITECTURE

In their memorandum on reform of the United Nations Organization, Brian Urquhart and Erskine Childers refer to the many 'superstitions' that have affected the running of the world body. They instance the initial refusal to site the headquarters building in Geneva because of the memory of the failure and impotence of the League. This is one superstition, then, for which we might be thankful. Anyone who has ever attended a session at the glacial *Palais des Nations* (as I once had to do in the course of Dr David Owen's protracted failure of nerve in the matter of turning Rhodesia into Zimbabwe) will appreciate that there is something hopelessly antithetical about the city which belongs as much to Calvin as to Rousseau. New York was the only possible city in which such an enterprise as the United Nations could have been launched. It is by definition and *par excellence* the first city of modernism. And something more than that: it is also, as a city, the apotheosis of internationalism. (Outstripped in both these respects to some extent by Los Angeles, it can still claim to be the superior of that metropolis in point of democracy, vigorous traditions of political struggle and historical weight.) It had once been a revolutionary capital. It was also the other end of the span which connected the Old World to the New. And the Old World, still under the ruins of Fascism, had scant choice but to look across the Atlantic and away from the Munichs, Sèvres, Versailles and Genevas which had been the scenes of its disgrace and very nearly of its suicide. San Francisco was an admirable place for a preparatory meeting (Alger Hiss in the chair) while the war was still being fought. Long Island is an excellent resort for discussions and conferences of what might be called a weekend nature, such as took place in the boskage of Lake Placid. But New York, and specifically Manhattan, was where it had to be.

A single anecdote may serve as a point of departure. The New York architect Wallace K. Harrison, who emerged as chief architect of the United Nations building, was compelled to listen to many designers and many lobbyists as well as many politicians. Here is how he came to include a dome in the rather awkward design of the General Assembly roof. The founding Secretary-General of the UN, Trygve Lie (of whom more later), encountered a budgetary crisis. Turning as usual to Washington for its solution, and asking for a government loan, he encountered a stipulation that was at once aesthetic and political. In Wallace Harrison's own words, reporting the exchange to his colleagues: 'According to Senator Austin, if you're going to get this loan request through Congress, the building should have a dome.'[1]

The dome is the special symbol of Capitoline self-regard throughout the United States. There is the imposing dome over the Congress itself on which work was continuing throughout the Civil War. Many state Capitols press rival claims – from Little Rock, Arkansas, to Lincoln, Nebraska, to Madison, Wisconsin (which claims a dome higher than Washington), to Hartford, Connecticut. Often the dimensions and scope of the dome are in an inverse ratio to the influence of the State. If it were not for the pride of the States, one sometimes thinks, the UN could as well have been titled the US, composed as it is of states rather than nations. But the hold on the title of *Estados Unidos* is, though not beyond dispute, almost as firm as the Northern hold on the title of 'America' itself. And American domination of the institution has been a feature from the first instalments of the design.

But what if we take the architecture of the Capitol itself as an analogy? When Washington was being laid out, the United States Constitution still inscribed as a matter of law the stipulation that the descendants of African slavery were only three-fifths human, and thus ineligible to vote or to own property. Indeed, for a time it mandated that they could be *held* as property. It withheld the franchise from adult females. Congress and the Supreme Court passed laws which further reinforced the domain of property rights over human rights. Yet by degrees and through bitter struggle and bloodshed, and still so far within the framework of the same Constitution and Court, the great roof of the Bill of Rights was expanded to include many more Americans and the children of immigrants who had not yet become Americans. Is it too fanciful to see, in the evolution of the United Nations, a comparable process of improvisation, expansion and amendment, such as to discover a greater *capacity* within the framework than had been originally mandated?

In asking, then, whether a great hall or palace designed by and for the mighty can become more than a waiting-room or an antechamber for the powerless, can transcend itself and become a place of justice and deliberation, it pays to attend to the floor-plan. In 1945, the reach of land between First Avenue and the East River and between Forty-Second and Fiftieth Streets was, like much of Old Europe, an abattoir. It formed a part of the real-estate empire of William Zeckendorf, Senior. The much-sought-after apartment buildings in today's mock-English location of Tudor City were in those days built without windows at the points where they overlooked the charnel-houses, and took in effluvia more reminiscent of Upton Sinclair or Lincoln Steffens than of riparian lightness and ease. But Mr Zeckendorf wanted, like many a tycoon before him, to be remembered for more than a few reeking stockyards. He wanted to create a memorial to himself in stone and glass. He conceived the idea of transforming his piece of Manhattan into another Rockefeller complex with opera house, concert hall and yachting marina all complete. The architect he chose was Wallace K. Harrison, who had worked on the mid-town Rockefeller Center. This was not to be the last imprint of the Rockefeller plutocracy on the design and location of the UN; that same Rockefeller plutocracy that had commissioned Diego Rivera to celebrate the family of man in murals on the original Center, only to remove them by chisel when they turned out to include scenes of insurgency and the iconic figure of Lenin. E.B. White composed an imaginary poetic dialogue between the billionaire and the artist which ended with Rockefeller exclaiming:

'And, after all, it's *my* wall.'

'*We'll see if it is*,' said Rivera.

The real-estate contest was conducted more sinuously on both sides this time and, for both sides, ended rather better. As the plans for the vast Zeckendorf Center matured in Harrison's office, and as it became plain that the new United Nations Organization might be contemplating the occupation of the very same site, George Dudley, of Mr Harrison's firm of Harrison and Abramowitz, simply took to a form of architectural double-entry bookkeeping, pencilling in the words 'General Assembly' where the opera house had been sited, or 'Security' or 'Trusteeship' in place of different auditoria. This double-entry practice was necessary because even though a Preparatory Commission of the UN had decided that the international headquarters should indeed be built in the United States, no decision on location had been arrived at. Three distinct consultative groups were put into being: the Headquarters Commission, made up of delegates and architects and chaired by Sir Angus Fletcher; the Committee on Sites and General Questions, chaired by the

Uruguayan delegate Juan Felipe Yriart; and the Headquarters Advisory Committee, chaired by the first American Permanent Representative to the UN, Senator Warren Austin of Vermont (he of the dome fixation).

To review the differing options and structures that were considered and discarded in this process (in meetings scrupulously minuted and preserved by George Dudley) is to glimpse a fragment of the history of possibility. One can glance in real time down roads that were not taken, and see again how architecture is the most revealing of the arts.

At the very first it was simply a matter of closing off certain options that would have placed the United Nations in a setting of isolation. The architect Robert Moses, a capitalist megalomaniac of Randian proportions who, in the rest of his career, was to immolate so much of New York to the automobile and the freeway, exploited his connection to the Rockefeller family, the city bureaucracy and the *New York Times* to seize the initiative with a blue-chip committee of his own. This body's objective was to site the UN at Flushing Meadow on Long Island, where Moses had enjoyed great success with his selection of the site for the 1939 World's Fair. As his biographer phrased it, where 'other men might see the formation of the United Nations in 1945 as a chance for peace, he saw it as a chance for a park'.[2] The submitted plan showed a cluster of long and low buildings grouped around a (domed) General Assembly and planted on the shores of an artificial lagoon.

This scheme did battle, in the selection process, with a plan to locate the headquarters either in the suburbs of Philadelphia (like New York a former capital of the United States), in the Presidio Park neighbourhood of San Francisco hard by the Golden Gate bridge, or in Fairfield County, Connecticut. The Philadelphia proposal never got past the drawing-board; the Pacific site, much favoured by the Australians and others, was vetoed by the USSR, and the Fairfield County proposal came to grief when UN prospectors were stoned by chauvinistic locals who mounted what was the first but by no means the last manifestation of American nativist resentment at 'World Government'.

In the event, after some further light skirmishing, a visit from three members of the Headquarters Commission determined that only the big city would do. (The three, incidentally, were Le Corbusier, Jan de Ranitz from the Netherlands, and a Soviet architect named Nikolai Bassov.) Although the Rockefeller family had supported the Robert Moses initiative it did not, in this crisis, forget the combination of suppleness and munificence which had made it famous. The United Nations desired a Manhattan command post? Why, in that case the Rockefellers would *give* it to them. With Wallace Harrison's ready mediation, Zeckendorf was found in the middle of a Lucullan party he was throwing for his own wedding anniversary and was offered $8.5 million in cash for the East River abattoirs. (On hearing that his father would sign this famous and later framed cheque on the spot, young Rockefeller is said to have exclaimed, 'Gee, Pop, that's swell.' Only Harrison failed to live up to the conventions of the rich man's club. Asked by Rockefeller to order champagne in quantity to celebrate the deal at once, he found that he had no money on his person.) By means of this rich, warm handshake, the United Nations 'took' the decision to start life on the East River, in the city of which Trotsky had written, during his brief sojourn as actor and activist, that it was: 'The foundry in which the fate of man is to be forged. . . . The fullest expression of our modern age, city of prose and fantasy, of capitalist automatism, its streets a triumph of cubism, its moral philosophy that of the dollar.' Peering beyond immediate impressions, he added: 'As I look enviously at New York – I who still think of myself as a European – I ask myself: "Will Europe be able to stand it? Will it not sink into nothing but a cemetery? And will the economic and cultural centres of gravity not shift to America?"'[3] He wrote this during the First World War, and by the time Europe had been turned twice into a cemetery the Rockefeller family had come to confirm him – never mind that irritating business about the Rivera mural – as 'objectively' prescient.

Formalities, such as tax exemption for the Rockefeller gift, did not take long to arrange. There arose the question of which architect – or perhaps we had better say which school of architecture – would best embody the new ideal. At first matters proceeded by a rough process of elimination which was in turn roughly, not to say crudely, congruent with the UN's founding circumstances. Thus the Finn Alvar Aalto, who was liked by Wallace Harrison, was disqualified because Finland had not met the conditions for UN membership (the salient one being that a country had to have declared war on the Axis by a certain deadline in 1945 – Turkey just getting in under the wire, with Ireland and Spain waiting for years to end their exclusion). Mies van der Rohe and Walter Gropius were deemed ineligible because of their German-ness – not, on the face of it, an aesthetic determination imbued with the spirit of internationalism. (While Mies, it is true, found the Third Reich a congenial working environment, the same could not be said of Gropius.) The finalized membership of the Board of Design showed the hallmarks of a later and institutional addiction of the UN in that it contained the widest possible spread of national member-ships with the least attention to individual character or distinction. But from this practice of the most consoling common denominator there were two exemptions. The first was Oscar Niemeyer of Brazil, whose Communist affiliations were to be a constant source of woe to him in the submission of ideas and, indeed, in his efforts to travel to New York. The second was the French-Swiss iconoclast Le Corbusier, author of the bold *Contemporary City for Three Million Inhabitants*, which he had extruded from his hyperactive imagination in 1922. (Both men had designed their countries' pavilions for the 1939 World's Fair.) Le

Corbusier was convinced – as was Wallace Harrison – that he had been wrongfully thwarted in the famous competition for the League of Nations headquarters design, held in Geneva in 1927. He met every definition of the loose cannon and never relaxed his vigilance in case of another collusion against his unfettered originality. Having at one point asserted: 'New York is a terrifying city. For us it is menacing. We are not wrong in keeping at a distance', and having further asserted that Long Island was hopeless because it would place the United Nations 'in the shadow of the skyscrapers of Manhattan',[4] he eagerly embraced the Manhattan scheme of the Rockefellers on the grounds that it would afford the ideal site for his original high-density plan of 1922! Clearly he intended to be in at the birth, no matter what the paternity.

The price of the Rockefeller benefaction was to be paid in *limitation*. Given the acreage of the East River abattoirs, on an island where the very scarcity of land had necessitated the innovation of the skyscrapers (using 'their full height to proclaim', as W.H. Auden put it, 'the strength of collective man'), there existed the perfect rationale for a minimal UN. Not only was the anticipated membership to be kept in low figures for design purposes, but also the bureaux of the essential ancillary institutions – World Court, International Labour Organization, Food and Agriculture, and the rest of the organization's viscera – could plausibly be decentralized and farmed out to ambitious peripheral capitals. Evidently something more than a judgement of taste and proportion was under consideration here.

We know of a number of attempts to make the layout more capacious or – which could have been the same thing – more concentrated. Ssu-ch'eng Liang, the Chinese member of the Board of Design, proposed a trapezoid layout with an oriental garden in the middle; an essentially contemplative model with the bowed shoulders turned away in a monastic attitude from the roar of the metropolis. The British member of the team, Howard

Robertson, inclined to the same concept, but for different reasons. Like many of his countrymen he thought of 'the quad' as the proper locus for serious reflection, and dilated fondly on the concept of the interior courtyard. By contrast, Sven Markelius of Sweden, who had been the planner of Stockholm, drew an almost Wallensteinian plan which threw a bridge across to Roosevelt Island and created a city within the city for a vast number of UN employees. He, too, was overruled. Somewhere in the contest over these competing designs, the Organization decided to become both micro- and megalocephalic: a head both too small and too large to issue, or to receive, the complex network of signals from its ganglia and limbs.

In the inception and execution of the headquarters project, in other words, one may 'read' the compromises and special interests that have so strongly marked the institution ever since. Robert Moses, the Parks Commissioner of the City, seized control of a plan which he had originally opposed. Disappointed by Congress and by the International Bank, the first Secretary-General, Trygve Lie (himself the essence of the superpower 'compromise candidate' and once described by Isaac Deutscher as the very figure of the deferential, unprincipled Social Democrat), resolved on a cramped and ungenerous UN. He told Wallace Harrison that the Secretariat building would have to come down by six floors – from forty-five to thirty-nine, in a bizarre reversal of the dates of the Second World War. The General Assembly was confined to one hall instead of two, and the conference and committee rooms of the complex were reduced by four. Public access and 'circulation' areas were shrunk commensurately. Le Corbusier was sent home by Lie with a flea in his ear, having insisted to the last that he could oversee a more ample and more intricate design.

Not everything, however, proceeded on this niggardly scale. The UN project had about it something of the scope and generosity of the New Deal, and kindled an equivalent emotion among democratic New Yorkers. Construction workers, who are among the folk-heroes of the city, demonstrated an enthusiasm not merely for the job but for the idea. Citizens felt themselves to be part of something large and ambitious. Yet the shadow of the Cold War was pressing in. The first premonition came with the Korean War and the sudden shortage of steel, when Wallace Harrison was compelled to remind the steel producers that they had undertaken not to raise the price of their product to a profiteer's level. Fernand Léger, who had been commissioned by Harrison to provide the murals for the hall of the General Assembly, was forbidden to enter the United States to realize the work. (In a somewhat bizarre echo of the Rivera controversy, Nelson Rockefeller agreed to pay Léger's fee and to deputize an art student to execute the designs by proxy.) They are still viewable today, none the better for this commission by remote control. So are the ventilation ducts on the interior of the delegates' lounge – an interior prefiguration of the exoskeleton of the Pompidou/Beaubourg excrescence. Sculpture by Henry Moore and Barbara Hepworth was also garnered by Harrison, but with less controversy. The spirit of Bloomsbury could be more safely annexed than the ethos of Communism. (It was not known until many years later that Mr Trygve Lie had fired a number of American employees for exercising their Constitutional right to plead the Fifth Amendment in the face of early anti-Communist inquisition, nor was it disclosed that he had allowed the FBI to insinuate itself into the Secretariat and to conduct within its diminished precincts the business of politicized and secret invigilation of civil servants, known as the 'loyalty' oath.)

The League of Nations – to revert once more to the impress made by superstition – had been believed to have failed because the United States had refused to endorse its charter or adhere to its membership. There was, therefore, a sort of double victory involved in the choice of New York as the 'workshop for peace', in Wallace Harrison's words. The United States had not just firmly anchored the United Nations to itself, but had firmly anchored itself to the charter of the United Nations. (This gave point to the later rallying cry of the McCarthyite and Birch Society extremists, who would yell in their conspiratorial pamphlets and speeches, 'US out of UN! UN out of US!') The price paid for host country status was, however, a certain American presumption of superiority, as what had been promiscuously called 'The American Century' met its halfway point.

Having begun the Second World War as an isolationist power, the United States concluded it as the greatest imperial power in world history; inheritor of bankrupt British and French colonialism and also the world's treasurer, as well as the only nuclear state on the planet and the possessor of the mightiest conventional arsenal. Indeed, Nelson Rockefeller and Wallace Harrison had already worked together, in President Roosevelt's office of the Co-ordinator of Inter-American Affairs, in consummating this outcome. The triumphally *American* character of the UN design was to become emulated for its own sake, as Victoria Newhouse notes in her book on Wallace Harrison:

> A year after the Secretariat was completed, Gordon Bunshaft produced the all-glass-walled Lever House on Park Avenue and Fifty-fourth Street. Within five years glass towers were rising across the United States and around the world. The building that may have lacked eloquence as a symbol of world peace became one of the most influential progenitors of American technology at the service of bureaucratic efficiency, and a true symbol of Western civilization at mid-century.[5]

Embedded somewhere in the ethos of this all-American success story, however, were the ideals of Oscar Niemeyer and the fragmentary *carnets de poche* scrawled by Le Corbusier, and lovingly preserved by George Dudley. Niemeyer and Le Corbusier, wrote

Sir Brian Urquhart, deserved more credit for the sweep of the final design than they have ever received. George Dudley points out drily that the placement of a wall of white marble at each end of the distinctive UN skyscraper makes it the most altruistic high-rise in New York because it forgoes, by its very nature, the most coveted of all executive and bourgeois status confirmations – the corner-window office. In the *carnets* of Le Corbusier appears the following tantalizing fragment, expressing a certain relation between form and content that has not, perhaps, been entirely obscured by subsequent overlays:

> We are laying down the plans of a world architecture, *world*, not *international*, for therein we shall respect the human, natural and cosmic laws. . . . There are no names attached to this work . . . there is simply discipline.

The same sort of reluctant conversion to the foreshortened workmanlike rendition of a sublime ideal seems to have overtaken other architects and other architectural critics as well. Only Frank Lloyd Wright was a consistent holdout and he, having been taken off the original Design Board by Wallace Harrison on the grounds that he was impossible to work with, may have had reasons for resentment. At any rate, his withering remark is worth minuting. He said of the Secretariat building that it was 'a glorification of negation. A deadpan box with no expression of the nature of what transpires within the building.'[6] More interesting was the series of appraisals penned by Lewis Mumford, who began by rating the entire project extremely low, and came to be won over despite himself. His first observation was more in the nature of a professional diagnosis, accurately describing the incipient buildings as 'a combination of Le Corbusier's breezy City of the Future and the businesslike congestion of Rockefeller Center, a blending of the grandiose and the obvious'.[7] There was, added Mumford, 'plenty of unconscious symbolism in what has happened so far'.

Because Mr Bernard Baruch was once a Wall Street man, it was probably bad symbolism to let him head up our Atomic Energy Delegation to the United Nations, even though he was daring enough to support a plan for socializing atomic energy on a world scale. And it was bad symbolism to let Mr Rockefeller get mixed up with the United Nations headquarters. Mr Rockefeller is a benevolent philanthropist who at one moment restores forgotten Colonial capitals and at another presents the City of New York with a handsome public park. But to some of our more difficult brothers overseas, Mr Rockefeller is Monopoly Capitalism, and the fact that it was he, and not the City of New York or the federal government, who gave this site to the United Nations will not, unfortunately, lessen their suspicions and animosities.[8]

With no less acuity, even though he did not know of the coming dispersal of UN functions and offices, let alone the future expansion of the Organization's membership, Mumford wrote in *The New Yorker*:

With great reluctance – indeed, with pain and embarrassment – I must cast a negative vote. Symbolically, these buildings are far from being an admirable expression of the idea of the United Nations, and functionally, they do not make the necessary provisions for extension, change of purpose, and future development.[9]

Drawing on the darker side of twentieth-century political architecture, he deplored the absence of a human scale and the lack of a 'transition from the intimate to the monumental'. And he condemned the decision to make the Secretariat structure the centre-piece, rather than the debating and deliberative chambers:

If the Secretariat Building will have anything to say as a symbol it will be, I fear, that the managerial revolution has taken place and that bureaucracy rules the world. I am sorry that the architects have apparently taken Mr James Burnham's discouraging thesis as an axiom, for the United Nations is an attempt to make other ideas prevail.[10]

Mumford looked back to the pre-modern ambitions of Sir Joseph Paxton's Crystal Palace and Sir Ebenezer Howard's Garden City, where the use of glass and steel prefigured the integration of light, air and space into a quotidian life hitherto deprived of them. He appreciated, even though he found it architecturally naïve, Mies van der Rohe's plan for a pristine all-glass skyscraper on a fragile steel basketry. Yet he worried that the UN construction was at once too modern and not modern enough:

> In the Assembly Building, as in the Conference Building, *the future is frozen solidly in the form of the present.* This lack of flexibility is a serious failure in planning for an institution that may undergo many constitutional changes before it solidifies into a durable mold.[11] (emphasis added)

The rather dilapidated and worn aspect disclosed by Adam Bartos's accompanying photographs, as well as the toll exacted by time and by compromise, lends point to Mumford's early observations. However, it should not be overlooked that he saw in some dimensions of the design a transcendent possibility. Writing, so to speak, against his own pessimism, Mumford conceded:

> No building in the city is more responsive to the constant play of light and shadow in the world beyond it; none varies more subtly with the time of day and the way the light strikes, now emphasizing the vertical metal window bars, now emphasizing the dark green of the spandrels and underlining the horizontality of the composition. No one had ever conceived of building a mirror on this scale before, and perhaps no one guessed what an endless series of pictures that mirror would reveal.[12]

This almost accidental tribute to an unforeseen quality is as near, perhaps, as one can come to a point of balance. Gathered around the cradle of the infant United Nations were the usual attendants of power that seek to shape institutions. *Realpolitik* in the form of victorious powers seeking to codify their own ascendancy. *Realpolitik*, too, in the form of a struggle for mastery between those very powers. Greed and pelf in the shape of a robber-baron dynasty cloaked in philanthropic guise. An assumption that there would quite literally be no seats at the table for the *damnés de la terre*. The awful preponderance of nuclear weaponry and other armaments in the allocation of hierarchy. The enshrinement of bureaucracy as the principle of administration. But withal, an elusive ghost in the machine.

The United Nations was defined in a war which, while it was certainly an imperialist war, was also a war against Fascism. It derived its founding charter and instruments from the elevated language of all preceding declarations of the rights of man. It bound its members, however cynical their policies and regimes, to uphold a standard of conduct that would once have seemed laughably Utopian. And it created a small acreage of international territory on the bank of a river in humanity's most recent urban Utopia and dystopia – the welcoming and pitiless city of New York, whose harbour was still bracketed by the immigration pens of Ellis Island and by the plinth of the Statue of Liberty. Architecture materializes the contradictions.

2

ACCIDENT AND DESIGN

In November 1993, one hundred and ten member states of the United Nations proposed a resolution which called upon the World Court to declare nuclear weapons illegal. To be precise, the combined membership of the Non-Aligned Movement petitioned the General Assembly of the world body to seek an advisory opinion from the International Court of Justice – known in the vernacular as the World Court – on the lawfulness of the use, or the threatened use, of thermonuclear devices. 'Laws', wrote the Scythian philosopher Anacharsis, 'are like cobwebs. They are strong enough to hold the weak, but too weak to hold the strong.' This ancient truth had not prevented the World Court, which sits in The Hague, from finding in favour of Nicaragua, for example, when that country asked for relief from a campaign of ruin and sabotage mounted by the United States government in the early 1980s. (The Reagan administration blandly announced that it would refuse to recognize either the decision or the Court, yet its own lawlessness finally landed it in at least some difficulty both at home and abroad.)

Supporting the resolution of the Non-Aligned Movement (NAM) were a number of influential non-governmental organizations (NGOs in the acronymic parlance of international meetings) such as International Physicians for the Prevention of Nuclear War.

Over time, many such bodies have attained observer status at the UN and, though often derided as the 'stage army of the good', have none the less come to exert a tangible and intangible moral influence. For a comparative example, ask yourself, Do the deliberations of the Norwegian Storting never recall the work of Hendryk Ibsen? Well, yes, you may say. But does it make no difference when Nelson Mandela, say, is made a Nobel Laureate?

A striking – not to say arresting – fact about the permanent members of the United Nations Security Council is that all of them have at their disposal weapons of planetary extinction. The French government of François Mitterrand, indeed, made this ugly pre-eminence into a pretend virtue when arguing, in the wake of the revolutionary events of 1989, that unified Germany should not be allotted a seat on the Security Council. The said Council, reasoned the Quai d'Orsay, was a nuclear club, and would be destabilized by the admission of an irresponsibly non-nuclear member. (The same objection was presumed to hold in the case of Japan.)

Now for an international body that was constituted on the basis of victory over German and Japanese Fascism, and further constituted on the effective demilitarization of both those countries, to argue in this way might be thought of as hypocritical or egotistic. All those who regard UN deliberations as a charade are entitled to take note of this extreme imbalance, which reserves the literal power of life and death to a handful of wealthy nations who have the further privilege of a voting system weighted in their favour. None the less, in order for this modest and symbolic measure to be defeated, it was necessary for the axiomatic superpowers to exert themselves more than a little. The NAM happens to require a unanimous vote of its members in order to forward any course of action. Within the ranks of the NAM, the axiomatic superpowers can usually discover a client state or two. In this case, Indonesia – which relies on the United States to protect it from international pressure over East Timor and other matters – joined with one Anglophone former African colony and one Francophone former colony in order to stall the NAM initiative.

Had the resolution gone forward, however, there might have been some intriguing consequences. The new Prime Minister of Canada, Jean Chrétien, had provisionally committed his party to support the World Court initiative. The Foreign Affairs Commission of the Italian Senate had passed a unanimous motion calling upon the Italian government to back the resolution if it were put to the General Assembly. The equivalent committee of the Irish Parliament in Dublin endorsed a similar call. In both these cases, the governments concerned evinced a willingness to follow the letter and spirit of the resolution. Meanwhile, the World Health Organization in Geneva passed a similar resolution through its governing body, the World Health Assembly, and continues to campaign for a binding legal decision from the World Court on the criminalization of nuclear arsenals. The so-far successful rearguard actions of the Five – Britain, Russia, France, the United States and China – seem increasingly like the petulance of a clique that has lost its charisma.

I select this one example to illustrate the situation that has been created by the end of the Cold War bipolar system, and by the expansion of United Nations membership, *and* by the larger role and capacity of non-state organizations on the periphery of the UN. The ambassador of an axiomatic superpower has more to do these days than uphold his country's supremacy by the lofty exercise of a veto. In the councils of the UN itself, he or she will have to argue for the continuation of an eclipsed 'Big Five'. In the committees of the same body he will be met with demands that Security Council membership be enlarged or even determined by election and rotation. In the lobbies and corridors and lounges he will be buttonholed by representatives of the Helsinki Citizens' Assembly, or the International Physicians for the Prevention of Nuclear War, or of Amnesty International, some of whom have won the Nobel Prize and all of whom have gradually won their right to be there and to be consulted.

Then again we might consider the annual *UN Human Development Report*, which seeks to qualify or correct the international league tables put out by the World Bank by taking account of life expectancy, literacy and income distribution in its ranking of the different countries in the world. In the 1994 issue it is noted that the cost of 28 missiles purchased by South Korea from the United States would have paid for the immunization of 12,000 children – and could have furnished safe water for three years for the 3.5 million Koreans who lack it. In the overall ranking the 1994 *Report* shows Canada number one in the average well-being of its citizens, followed by Switzerland, Japan, Sweden and Norway. However, an alternative chart gives an alternative order, if due weight is given to gender discrepancies. If disparate treatment of the sexes is taken into account, Japan plummets sixteen places, the United States four. The *UN Human Development Report* could, no doubt, adopt even more stringent criteria for evaluating member states, but it is valuable that it seeks to do so at all.

The possibilities of such creative tension have been latent since the foundation of the UN. In pursuit of a world order which they would control, 'the powers' agreed to a formal surrender of some authority to a metaphysical forum that was, in some sense, *supra-national*. It partook, in this respect, of an old and somewhat ambivalent agitation in favour of 'world government' as something distinct from international co-operation. The authoritarian Fabianism of H.G. Wells and George Bernard Shaw, which envisaged a species of world *state*, found an echo in the more gentle and herbivorous campaigns of inter-war bodies like the Union of Democratic Control and Nobel Peace laureates like Sir Norman Angell, who looked for a consensus strong enough to outlaw war. This semi-pacifist style was obliterated morally by the ditherings of the League and the perception that insufficient 'hardness' had been demonstrated by the democracies in the face of Fascism. But the Utopian view was to recombine with the authoritarian in the period immediately following the Nuremberg verdicts and the UN proclamations. Albert Einstein, for instance, began by proposing a 'World Government' where 'the legislative assembly of the United Nations must be composed of men and women who are responsible not to national governments but only to the people who elect them'. The General Assembly, said Einstein in a celebrated broadcast, would thus determine the Security Council instead of the other way about, and the veto power of the few would be eliminated. In a subsequent (1947) 'Open Letter to the General Assembly', Einstein faced the likelihood that the Soviet Union, for one, might not wish to join such a General Assembly. In that contingency, he wrote, the only solution would be 'a *partial* world government which would have to be very strong . . . comprising at least two-thirds of the major industrial and economic areas of the world'[13] (emphasis added). He cautioned that such a partial world government should never 'act as an alliance against the rest of the world'. Here one can see the tendency of idealism to become dogmatic when thwarted.

In point of fact, the United Nations did begin life as a 'partial world government'. The United States insisted upon seating its Taiwanese clients as the representatives of the whole of China (rather as if, Tom Driberg once remarked, envoys to England were to be accredited to the Dame of Sark instead of to the Court of St James). It also enlisted many of its Latin American client states as full members, which prompted a no less bogus claim on the part of Stalin that Ukraine and Belorussia be granted membership as an independent state. Meanwhile the greater part of humanity was without any delegate at all. And, so far from outlawing war, the UN began to regulate and codify its applications. Even before Korea, where the United Nations actually went to war in its own name, it had discovered that the world was a dangerous place. Perhaps the best metaphor here was the murder on 17 September 1948 of the UN mediator in Palestine, Count Folke Bernadotte. Bernadotte was a Swede, and Sweden had been neutral in the Second World War and thus ineligible for early membership. But his work alongside Raoul Wallenberg in the rescue of European Jewry under the Swedish diplomatic flag had at first recommended him as a negotiator with the emerging Jewish state that had actually been created by a United Nations resolution. His assassins, moreover, proved to be the leaders of the underground which had brought that state into existence. (Their chief, Yitzhak Shamir, was later to become Israel's Prime Minister.) Unable to despatch more than a handful of 'monitors' to the region to underwrite the efforts of the equivocal Ralph Bunche, the UN was thus faced very early on with the realization that it had no troops to call its own, and that it could only count on powerful member states making troop commitments when they felt their own interests to be paramount. The Military Committee of the UN suffers from this want of authority to the present day.

Rather more important, but considerably less camera-worthy, has been the UN's role in helping to decide the balance of *economic* power in the globe. The politico-military and macro-economic dimensions of the embryo UN actually developed, as is often forgotten, in parallel. Thus, the germ was the Churchill–Roosevelt 'Atlantic Charter', endorsed by the fifteen nations in the anti-Hitler coalition while the struggle was in its incipient stages. On New Year's Day 1942, barely a month after the Hirohito attack on Pearl Harbor, an expanded coalition of twenty-six governments agreed on the first Declaration of 'the United Nations' (a phrasing put forward by Roosevelt himself) which anticipated a post-war system. In 1943 another meeting established the Food and Agriculture Organization (FAO), which was followed six months later by the founding of the United Nations Relief and Rehabilitation Administration (UNRRA). Thus even *in utero* the prospective body was supposed to concern itself with more than the arbitration of war and diplomacy. The critical contribution here, little-noticed at the time and little-regarded since, was made by John Maynard Keynes. In his *Proposals for an International Clearing Union*, composed in 1942, he showed himself also to be animated by the desire for a more just and rational post-war contract:

> We need a system possessed of an internal stabilizing mechanism, by which pressure is exercised on any country whose balance of payments with the rest of the world is departing from equilibrium *in either direction*, so as to prevent movements which must create for its neighbours an equal but opposite want of balance.[14] (original emphasis)

This essay, and others like it, became the outline of the Bretton Woods system, and the warrant for both the World Bank and the International Monetary Fund. Again, the over-arching design was one of increased equity, if not exact equality. But cautious as it was, and committed as it was from the first into the keeping of even more cautious hands, it marked an advance in principle over the economic anarchy of the 1930s. Keynes himself proposed that the Bank and the Fund (which in his conception would have included an International Clearing Union) should act as interventionist managers of the international economic system, and should do so *under resolutions established by the General Assembly*. If these thoughts were revolutionary then, how much more so are they now, as we enter the age of unstaunchable indebtedness.

It was this unfulfilled but still pregnant possibility of the UN that attracted the wrath and hatred of the American Right (and, depending upon how their own national myths were treated by the General Assembly, the subsequent resentment of the British Right over Suez, the Russian chauvinists in the Yeltsin period, the Israelis, the Iraqi Baathists, and others). The paranoid element in American politics was well summarized by the McCarthyite Senator William Knowland who, in an address at Georgetown University in 1957, described the Charter as a spider web in which his great country was enmeshed, and even invoked biblical authority for his rejection of the supra-national one. Reaching for Second Corinthians, he intoned: 'Be ye not unequally yoked together with unbelievers. For what fellowship has righteousness with unrighteousness and what communion has light with darkness?' In his fervid eagerness to disown any godless court of appeal which might or could overrule any autonomous decision of the United States – and being obsessed, as were many of his co-thinkers, with the role played by Alger Hiss in the original UN Secretariat – Senator Knowland failed to register the fact that the 'unequal' part of the equation operated in the reverse direction.

Part of the problem in matching the proclaimed ideals of the UN as an international arbiter to the more modest wishes of the powers that be and the more clamant needs of the oppressed has lain in the office of Secretary-General. In practice, if not by definition, the seeker of this post must be more than anything ready to consider himself, and to be considered by others, the very essence of 'the compromise candidate'. The first occupant of the position, Trygve Lie, asked rhetorically how it was that 'a Norwegian labour lawyer' had earned this onerous responsibility. Neither he nor anyone else ever came up with a remotely satisfactory answer to the question. (Conor Cruise O'Brien, in his spirited early work on the UN entitled *Sacred Drama*, drily evoked the quarrel between Lie and Soviet delegate Vyshinsky over Korea, recalling that 'both of them had played their parts, more than a decade before, in the long process of the destruction of the great tragic hero of the century, Leon Trotsky'. Vyshinsky, chief prosecutor in Stalin's Moscow trials, had bayed for Trotsky's blood while he was a political exile in Norway; Lie, in pursuit of a quiet life, had meekly acceded to demands for Trotsky's deportation. Thus is *realpolitik* consummated. The peoples of both North and South Korea paid a heavy price for the necessary illusion that both Mr Lie and Mr Vyshinsky were upholding matters of principle.)

Yet occupants of the Secretary-General's chair have also demonstrated the capacity to grow while in office, and not just to shrink or to remain paltry and mediocre. They have done so, even if only briefly, by using the international tribune as a place from which to recruit moral suasion. Thus when Dag Hammarskjöld rose to address the Security Council on 20 July 1960, to report that the United Nations 'itself' (not under a false flag this time) had decided to protect the newly won political independence of the Congolese people, he was able to rally support by designating:

> a turn of the road where our attitudes will be of decisive significance, I believe, not only for the future of the Organization but also for the future of Africa. And Africa may well in the present circumstances mean the world.[15]

Not many months later, the public galleries of the UN erupted in a furious demonstration at the news of the foul murder of Patrice Lumumba. But at least for an instant, Hammarskjöld had succeeded in shaming the international community into an attitude of responsibility. In his foreword to Hammarskjöld's book *Markings*, W.H. Auden remembered that the late Secretary-General had once told him that the job 'is like being a secular Pope and the Papal throne is a lonely eminence'.[16] Especially with its evocation of the old 'how many divisions?' question, this has an element of pathos – as did Trygve Lie's lame suggestion that the UN troops sent to Korea under General Douglas MacArthur be defined as an 'international brigade'. Still, the importance of the symbolic and the principled can be demonstrated just as keenly in the negative as in the positive; in their absence as well as in their brief presence.

Not unlike, it might be argued, the role of character in the American Presidency, the UN 'SG' has the power to create a certain atmosphere, emphasize a certain theme, stress a certain note and in general operate at the top as well as the bottom of the Weberian register of authority – the leaderly and spontaneous as well as the official and the routine. U Thant's combination of diffidence and stoicism throughout the Vietnam War may have appeared fatalistic to some – I remember it did to me – but taken in the long view, it seems to have augmented the dignity of the office. The hawk-faced opportunism and spurious even-handedness of Kurt Waldheim were superbly suited to a disastrous period of late-Cold War stalemate and stupidity, and seemed apt for the times even before the revelation of Waldheim's mendacity about his past. Peruvian and Egyptian successors, evidently cushion-like in their readiness to take the impression of whoever last sat upon them, have helped to define a period of flux and indecision during the meltdown of once-formative allegiances.

I ventured earlier an oblique comparison between the Constitutions of the United States and the United Nations, with the concomitant struggle to fill the spare capacity being delineated by the generosity of the wording. 'We, the people . . . ' begins the preamble to the United States Constitution. 'We, the peoples . . . ' begins the Charter of the UN in noticeable contrast to the League of Nations preamble, which spoke haughtily of 'We, the High Contracting Parties'. How, then, to fill the promised space? Not merely with words, even though the Charter goes on to declaim magnificently about 'the equal rights of men and women and of nations large and small,' and the promotion of 'social progress and better standards of life in larger freedom', to say nothing of 'friendly relations among nations based on respect for the principle of equal rights and self-determination of peoples'. Not all the residue of five decades' revulsion from platitude can quite strip these sentences of their context, or their lustre.

I happened to be writing these paragraphs in the week when Nelson Mandela became the first true President of South Africa in that country's first genuine election. I also happened to be rereading Conor Cruise O'Brien's personal memoir of the United Nations, *Sacred Drama*, cited above. In a brilliant piece of dialectical reasoning, O'Brien (writing almost three decades ago, and before his own conversion to *Realpolitik*) showed how those who disbelieved in the United Nations' power to deploy exemplary and unarmed force were not such practical persons as they seemed. Having shown without difficulty that both the United States and Great Britain had been defenders of the South African position at the UN – either for reasons of trade or for reasons of anti-Communism, or for some combination of the two – O'Brien spent some enjoyable time satirizing the positions of both Security Council members on Rhodesia and South West Africa (Namibia). What were the angry votes of the African delegates, and their clumsily worded resolutions against 'racism' and 'colonialism', set against this serene exercise in the management of the status quo? Well, argued O'Brien with suggestive and dangerous patience:

> Some 'friends of South Africa' comfort themselves with the thought that the pressures which are unmistakably developing are of no consequence, being merely rhetorical and legalistic. The power of the South African army and police is real: that of the United Nations symbolic only. This is a common-sense view, but a short-sighted one; it is natural and consistent that 'the friends of

South Africa' should underestimate the role of the imagination in politics and overestimate that of the police.[17]

Having pointed out that Britain and the USA had casually voted for a few resolutions which commanded their adherence to larger principles, O'Brien tried to explain what happens when people sign an ethical cheque which they do not believe will ever fall due:

> Rhetoric has its own dynamics, and the dynamics of a rhetoric which involves arguments of international law – when such arguments are used by those who have means to impose their concepts of international law – are powerful and dangerous. The 'power of the United Nations', and in particular of the General Assembly, is the power to evoke such rhetoric and squeeze it towards action. The legal rhetoric of a great power is a commitment, though a loose one, and this is especially so of a great power in which a government, not in control of the press and other media, has continually to persuade its own public opinion that it is doing the right thing. Once certain words have been spoken, the justifications, which must accompany future action or inaction, have been partly predetermined. And if the justifications are partly predetermined so also are the limits of action.[18]

It involves no disrespect to the freedom-fighters of Southern Africa to say that this piece of argument accurately prefigured the fashion in which their oppressors became subject to international isolation – an isolation finally consummated in the age of Thatcher and Reagan, which is surely more than even O'Brien would have ventured to foresee.

Other pillars of might have melted like snow, and will melt yet. The epoch of post-Cold War and post-Gulf War is, however, neither a post-war era nor an era free of non-military threats to peace. Is there a chance that the solvent power of rhetoric and principle, as adumbrated above, can compact with new institutions and new relationships in order to ensure that outcomes like the South African one can be encompassed rather sooner, and owe rather less to luck?

Or one might instance the rather moving scene described by Michael Doyle and Nishkala Suntharalingam (in the journal *International Peacekeeping*), in their treatment of the discharge of the mandate of UNTAC, the small force which oversaw the elections in Cambodia. With a staff of 7,000 raw civilians and 15,000 troops, and an estimated budget of $1.5 billion over eighteen months, UNTAC could not do everything. Indeed, the authors specifically fault it for failing to demobilize all the militias, some of them supported from outside, which had ravaged Cambodia since the 'Year Zero' calamity of the mid-1970s. However, UNTAC was able to recruit and train 50,000 Cambodian poll workers, establish 2,000 polling stations and provide an assurance of limited security for voters. 'It is no exaggeration', the authors record, 'to say that the courage of Cambodia's voters rescued UNTAC from what appeared to be a looming disaster.' In the face of what it would be euphemistic to anyone with a sense of recent history to describe as mere 'intimidation', a full 90 per cent of the Cambodian electorate voted.

Here was a nation which had endured the very worst that the Cold War could do to it, from carpet-bombing by the American empire to Stone Age Stalinism, and had yet responded when afforded the least encouragement. With minimal international guarantees, the population had reclaimed a place in history. The credit might be theirs – indeed, it is theirs, as it is in South Africa and elsewhere. But the role of certain international *norms* – to give them an arid name – of human rights and self-determination and democratic procedure has thereby regained some of the credit lost in Somalia, Bosnia and elsewhere.

3

AND THE FUTURE?

Were all humanity a single nation-state, the present North–South divide would make it an unviable, semi-feudal entity, split by internal conflicts. Its small part is advanced, prosperous, powerful; its much bigger part is underdeveloped, poor, powerless. A nation so divided within itself would be recognized as unstable. A world so divided should likewise be recognized as inherently unstable.[19]

Having to some extent rid itself of constraint – or perhaps we had better say the excuses for constraint – by surviving the Cold War paralysis and the Gulf War rictus and by contriving to assist in the baptism of one or two success stories, the United Nations now needs several sorts of amendment. It needs, specifically and urgently, to confront the following;

(1) Its budgetary beggardom, which is another way of saying its budgetary dependence on a small group of powers.
(2) Its role as the provider of 'international brigades' and the enforcer of last resort at the bar of international law.
(3) Its forgotten responsibility to impose some order and decency on the anarchy of the international terms of trade.

(4) Its mandate as the steward of human rights standards, not just between states and nations but also within them.

(5) Its own 'democractic deficit', which consists of two related shortcomings: first, the discrepancy between General Assembly and 'Permanent Five' states; and second, the distance between governmental and non-governmental participation.

In describing something of the debate that went on over the forty-five eventual schemes proposed for the original physical architecture of the UN, I used the phrase (which I owe to Perry Anderson) 'the history of possibility'. The same tantalizing reflection occurs when one surveys the founding moral and political architecture of the world body. The precedent model for a mutually verifiable and enforceable regime of agreed international standards was the International Labour Organization (ILO), a surviving relic of the qualified idealism of the League of Nations and the only branch of that body to which the United States ever officially adhered. The ILO, founded in Europe, removed itself to the United States during the Second World War and succeeded in raising a number of traditional workers' objectives to the level of international law. Just so, it was hoped and believed by some, the institutions of a United Nations would with some amplitude redress the causes and mitigate the effects of inequality among nations – if only for the utilitarian reason that such discrepancies had so often furnished the pretext of war. But even utilitarian proclamations must sometimes be couched in exalted language and there is always the chance of the language being interpreted literally . . .

Begin, then, by looking at the institutional format of the United Nations. Its principal organs were agreed to number six: the first being the governing body or General Assembly. Next came the Security Council, the Economic and Social Council (ECOSOC), the Trustees Council, the International Court of Justice (sometimes known as the World Court) and the Secretariat with its Secretary-General. At the first glance which falls upon this top deck of the UN hierarchy, it is very plain which of the six institutions is the orphan. Who has ever read a decision of ECOSOC, or listened to one of its debates?

The same international amnesia can be identified a little lower in the chain. Specialized bodies with tiny budgets, like the UN Children's Fund (UNICEF) or its refugee pro-gramme (UNHCR), are at least known for their quasi-charitable exertions, as is the World Health Organization or UNESCO or the FAO. But who really remembers that under the terms of the United Nations Charter, the so-called 'Bretton Woods' institu-tions – namely the IMF and the World Bank with their lending and financing subsidiaries – are part of the UN constellation?

This immense or potentially immense apparatus for providing an alternative to the dire situation that is correctly defined in the conclusions of the South Commission (cited above) was actually given a rubric in Article 55 of the Charter, which provided that the UN 'shall promote':

(a) higher standards of living, full employment, and conditions of economic and social progress and development;

(b) solutions of international economic, social, health and related problems, and inter-national cultural and educational cooperation; and

(c) universal respect for, and observance of, human rights and fundamental freedoms for all without distinction as to race, sex, language or religion.

Note, first, that it was the whole body and not any subsidiary branch or agency that was charged with implementing these objectives. Note, further, as Brian Urquhart and Erskine

Childers do in their 'Renewal' manifesto, that except for the omission of environmental questions the whole of Article 55 might have been drafted by today's idealists. Note, again, that the San Francisco founding conference of the UN adopted an understanding of what was meant by 'economic' in the words of Article 55. It was determined that 'economic' was to be interpreted to comprise international trade, finance, communications and transport, economic reconstruction, and international access to raw materials and capital goods. Yet when was the last time a member state invoked Article 55, as against the much better known Article 51 (providing for the unilateral right of self-defence)? In effect, all of the subsequent failures, anomalies and inequalities can be traced to this original one.

Urquhart and Childers provide a useful table of comparison, illustrating the different principles that now govern the UN proper and the World Bank/IMF. The crucial differences lie in the attitude to membership, which in the first case (that of the UN) is granted to any state which agrees to abide by UN principles, and in the Bank/Fund case is subject to financial subscription and other economic criteria. The rule at the UN is one member one vote; at the Bank/Fund, voting is weighted according to shares. UN Development assistance takes the form of grants or of the lowest long-term interest rates, while Bank/Fund terms are at the full market rate with very few exceptions.

Erskine Childers, who was formerly Senior Advisor to the Director-General of the UN for Development and International Economic Cooperation, has phrased the dilemma in the following bold style:

> Not one specialized-agency headquarters has been located at the UN. The United States smashed all hope of an equitable world trade system – the key to advancement of all peoples – by

blocking the creation of the International Trade Organization. All we got instead was the General Agreement on Tariffs and Trade, which should have been called the *Specific* Agreement to continue the Imperial Trading System. It has never covered trade vital to the poor countries. In the Uruguay Round key Northern countries negotiated virtually among themselves for seven years, then gave the South *one weekend* to consider their draft document.

Address to the NCO Conference on Development and Conflict: The Hague, February 1994

The Urquhart–Childers document proposes a number of steps to close the gap between diplomacy and political economy in the scope of the UN. The simplest and most daring of these proposals takes the form of an 'Economic Security Council' to transcend ECOSOC and to hold yearly meetings at which all states would discuss and defend their trade policies in the open. At present, the tendency is rather in the opposite direction. In 1992, indeed, Mr Boutros Boutros Ghali peremptorily abolished the post of Director-General for Development, underscoring the low value placed on the subject by the senior powers of the world body.

Inseparable from any consideration of this question is the budgetary structure of the UN itself. Currently the Organization is $2.23 billion in arrears of member-state contributions. Of this figure, $598 million was owed by the Russian Federation and $834 million by the United States. The second delinquency is in some ways the more reprehensible, since the United States is the host country and since, according to the City Government of New York, the greater New York region takes in approximately $800 million annually in UN-generated income. But taken together, the default by the two former Cold War colossi is a reflection of a wider arrogance which arises only in part from the fact that Permanent Members of the Security Council, since they are not elected from the General Assembly, cannot be stripped of their voting privileges.

Reflecting the isolationist tendencies which helped bring him to high office, President Clinton has proposed from the podium of the UN that the United States contribution be reduced in any case. (He has also retreated from the call for a permanent UN-commanded independent peace-keeping force, which formed part of his election platform.) Some see in this parsimony an occasion to reduce the dependence of the UN on its richest and most powerful member. Suggestions for giving the UN an income of its own range from a tax on international arms sales to a levy on the Law of the Sea treaty, by which the UN could retain a proportion of the vast franchises which will be awarded for exploitation of the ocean floor.

Some such declaration of financial independence and integrity will be necessary if the question of peace-keeping is ever to be addressed seriously. As Brian Urquhart has put it:

> From the comments of the press and national legislators, one might conclude that the UN and its operations are an unbearable financial burden. In fact, in 1992 the UN and all its peace-keeping forces throughout the world cost $2.4 billion – less than the cost of two days of Desert Storm or two Stealth bombers. The average ratio of UN peace-keeping assessments to national defence expenditures is of the order of one dollar to one thousand dollars.

This in turn means that peacekeeping operations notionally under UN control are hostage to the caprice of member-state commanders. A notorious example is that of Somalia, where the decision to deploy the US Rangers on 3 October 1993 in the disastrous incident which led to the deaths of many Somalis and eighteen Americans was actually taken by the US Joint Special Operations Command. This outfit is based in Tampa, Florida, and took no consultation with the UN HQ in Mogadishu. In the same month the United States Navy vessel which was carrying UN observers to Haiti took the unilateral decision to turn tail in the face of Haitian junta violence and bore the observers back with it. Only a force composed of volunteers (as are the Swedes, for example, in the Balkans) and free of member-state political pressures could hope to uphold an initial General Assembly or Security Council decision to become involved, and to act with the due despatch that in Haiti would certainly have made the difference. When the UN was founded Tom Winteringham, formerly Commander of the British battalion in the International Brigade in Spain and a founder of the Home Guard, urged that the organization needed its own independent military force – or 'World Guard', as he proposed calling it. Perhaps a less forbidding name could have been found, but essentially he was right.

An unspoken drawback of the peace-keeping system is the way that it underlines the already sharp inequalities between nations. As the Non-Aligned Movement resolution on nuclear weaponry reminds us, it is unthinkable that the power of the Security Council be brought to bear on any nuclear programme much larger than that of Iraq or North Korea. Thus the real consummation of all the proclaimed principles of 1944 and 1945 lies in a democratization of the UN itself. It has been proposed that a UN Parliamentary Assembly be set in motion, on the analogy of the European Parliament, to act as a counterweight to the entrenched powers of the Secretariat and the Permanent Five. By submitting the work of the unelected members of the Assembly to a Question Time and to second readings, this body could give direction to another source of potential vitality – the growing interest of non-governmental organizations. A committee of the Canadian House of Commons has already proposed that Canada host a preparatory meeting for a UN Parliamentary Assembly, while over the past few years an unusual volume of NGO activity has been pressing the UN to live up to its charter. There was the 1993 Human Rights Conference in Vienna and also the International Women's Conference, both of which were able to mobilize thousands of activists world-wide to lobby UN delegations concerning long-unkept promises on human rights and gender equality. Similar initiatives have been recognized and some of their members included in UN-sponsored high-level discussions of disarmament and the environment.

The history of international and multinational arbitration is not an especially inspiring one. The great deformity of the process has usually been its domination by the very powers whose greed and aggressiveness is the problem in the first place. (The first Hague Peace Conference was called by the Tsar of All the Russias and the second by Theodore Roosevelt.) Yet even the most hardened practitioners of *Realpolitik* can become convinced, not just of their own self-interest in international law, but also of the general human interest. While he was the American delegate in New York, Daniel Patrick Moynihan won himself a deserved reputation as a man of the most unsentimental, 'national interest' conservatism. Yet reflecting on his appointment in a later memoir he recorded:

> During my tenure as US Permanent Representative to the UN, Spanish Sahara was partitioned by Morocco and Mauritania, and Portuguese Timor was invaded and conquered by Indonesia. In both cases the United States was more than content that this should happen while the Soviet Union, in one instance, and the People's Republic of China, on the other, very much tried to prevent it. The notion of law no more entered *our* policy than it did *theirs*.

The belatedness of Moynihan's insight does little to rob it of its value. It remains for the secular forces of democracy, internationalism and citizen's initiative to stop waiting for an outbreak of goodwill among their betters and fill the battered vessel of the UN Charter with the revolutionary implications that it implicitly summons.

Notes

1. Interview between Victoria Newhouse and George Dudley, 9 April 1984, cited in Victoria Newhouse, *Wallace K. Harrison, Architect*, New York 1989, p. 130.

2. Robert A. Caro, *The Power Broker: Robert Moses and the Fall of New York*, New York 1975, p. 1085.

3. Leon Trotsky, *Novy Mir*, 1917; cited in *My Life: An Attempt at an Autobiography*, Harmondsworth 1975, p. 280.

4. Le Corbusier, *United Nations Headquarters Report*, New York 1946, pp. L8–20; cited in Newhouse, p. 115.

5. Newhouse, p. 143.

6. F.L. Wright, *The New York Times*, 24 July 1949; cited in Newhouse, p. 143.

7. Lewis Mumford, 'U.N. Model and Model U.N.', *The New Yorker*, 1947, reprinted in *From the Ground Up: Observations on Contemporary Architecture, Housing, Highway Building, and Civic Design*, New York 1956, p. 21.

8. Ibid., p. 25.

9. Mumford, 'Buildings as Symbols', *The New Yorker*, 1947, reprinted in *From the Ground Up*, p. 28.

10. Ibid., p. 30.

11. Mumford, 'United Nations Assembly', *The New Yorker*, 1953, reprinted in *From the Ground Up*, p. 59.

12. 'Magic with Mirrors', *The New Yorker*, 1951, reprinted in *From the Ground Up*, pp. 40–41.

13. Albert Einstein, 'An Open Letter to the General Assembly of the United Nations, on "the way to break the vicious circle" ', *United Nations World*, vol. I, October 1947, pp. 13–14.

14. John Maynard Keynes, 'Proposals for an International Clearing Union', April 1943; reprinted in Seymour E. Harris (ed.), *The New Economics: Keynes' Influence on Theory and Public Policy*, New York 1947, p. 326.

15. Dag Hammarskjöld, *Markings*, trans. Leif Sjoberg and W.H. Auden, London 1966; speech on 20 July 1960.

16. W.H. Auden, 'Markings', in *Forewords and Afterwords*, selected by Edward Mendelson, London 1973, p. 445.

17. Conor Cruise O'Brien and Feliks Topolski, *United Nations: Sacred Drama*, New York 1968, p. 52.

18. Ibid.

19. South Commission, *The Challenge to the South: Report of the South Commission*, under the chairmanship of Julius Nyerere, Oxford 1990, p. 2.

PHOTOGRAPHS

INTERNATIONAL TERRITORY

TERRITOIRE INTERNATIONAL

CORRIDOR TO CONFERENCE
BUILDING

SECRETARIAT BUILDING

RADIO AND TV STUDIOS, DIALS
TUNED TO DELEGATIONS'
BROADCASTS

S 3770, OFFICE OF
UNDERSECRETARY-GENERAL
FOR POLITICAL AFFAIRS

SECURITY DESK, VISITORS'
LOBBY

VISITORS' LOBBY, EAST

DELEGATES' MEETING AREA
G.A. BUILDING

SECOND-FLOOR CORRIDOR
G.A. BUILDING

CHESS CLUB, G.A. BUILDING

TRUSTEESHIP COUNCIL

G.A. BUILDING WEST

SPUTNIK, VISITORS' LOBBY

GENERAL ASSEMBLY AND
SECRETARIAT BUILDINGS

PRESS BAR, G.A. BUILDING

CONFERENCE BUILDING

ELEVATORS

SECRETARIAT LOBBY

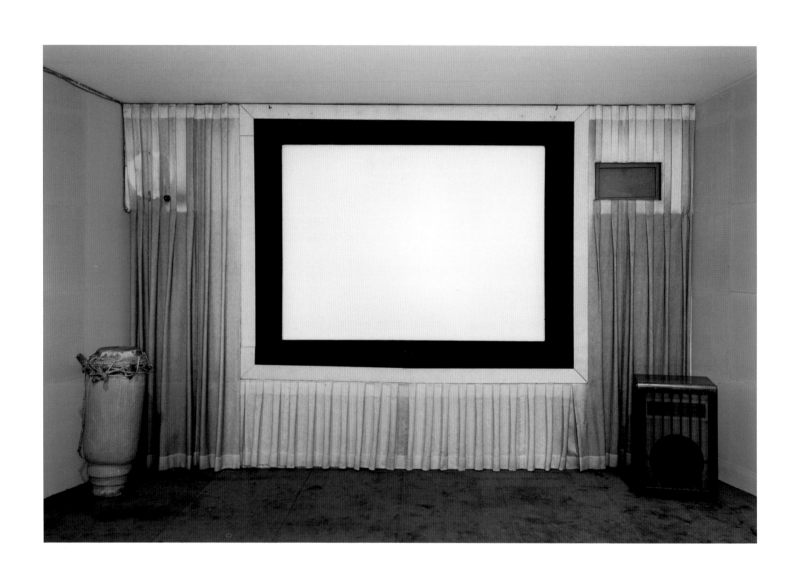

MOVIE THEATRE, SECRETARIAT
BUILDING

S 1446, RUSSIAN
TRANSLATION SERVICE

SECRETARY-GENERAL'S OFFICE

STUDIO SEVEN RADIO
CONTROL ROOM

CONFERENCE BUILDING
FROM EAST RIVER
PROMENADE

CONFERENCE BUILDING
AND QUEENS

EAST WALL, G.A. BUILDING

MOVIE THEATRE

MAP SECTION, LIBRARY

DELEGATES' DINING-ROOM

GYM

S 1494, SPANISH
TRANSLATION SERVICE

I.D. SECTION

S 2310, CHINESE BOOK CLUB

VISITORS' LOBBY, WEST

S 1445, RUSSIAN TRANSLATION
SERVICE

S 2314, CHINESE TRANSLATION
SERVICE

S 1477, SPANISH TRANSLATION
SERVICE

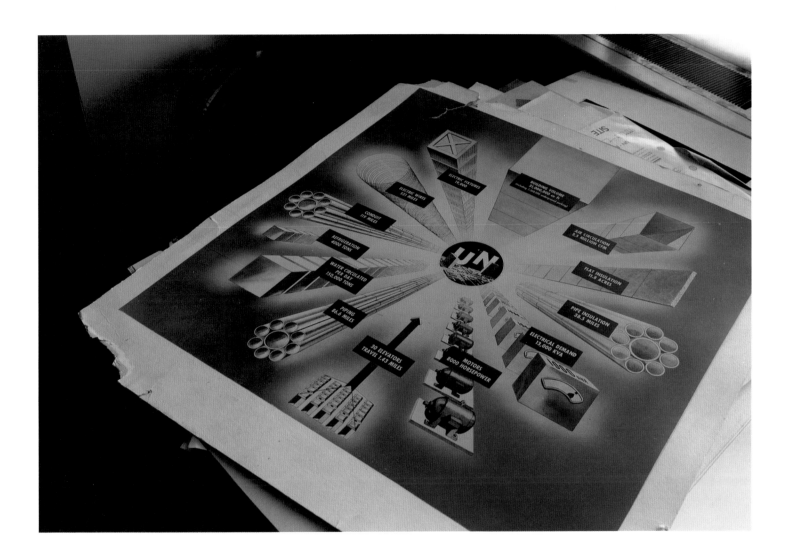

SECURITY COUNCIL

UNIFORM SECTION

S 1446, RUSSIAN TRANSLATION
SERVICE

PRESS 'BULL PEN'

DRIVEWAY, SCULPTURE BY
BARBARA HEPWORTH

DELEGATES' DINING-ROOM
ROOF

VISITORS' LOBBY CEILING

GENERAL ASSEMBLY
BUILDING SOUTH

G.A. 200, AIR VENT

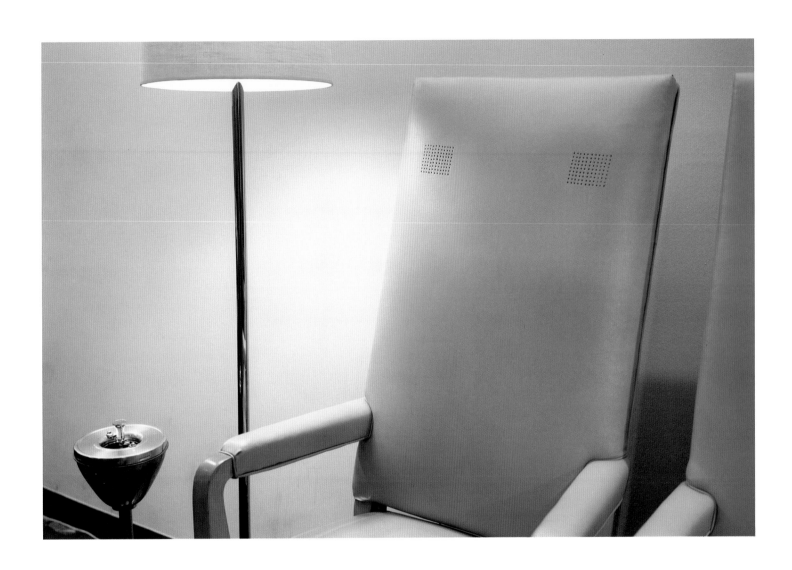

G.A. 200, CHAIRS WITH
SPEAKERS FOR TRANSLATION

SECURITY COUNCIL, MURAL
BY PER KROHG

JAPANESE PEACE BELL

MURAL BY FERNAND LEGER,
GENERAL ASSEMBLY EAST
WALL

GENERAL ASSEMBLY PODIUM

DELEGATES' ENTRANCE,
'TRIUMPH OF PEACE' GIFT
OF BELGIUM

DELEGATES' ENTRANCE

GENERAL ASSEMBLY

PHOTOGRAPHER'S NOTE

These pictures were taken from late in 1989 through 1993. The offices and elevators in the Secretariat are gradually being modernized but, as the viewer will see, what captivated me about the place was its evocation of the mid-century and its relatively untampered-with condition.

I am very grateful to the late Pedro Guillen, Chief of the Media Accreditation and Liaison Unit of the Department of Public Information, whose enthusiastic and freewheeling support of this project made it possible in the early stages; and the present staff, including Sonia Lecca, Chief, and Public Information Assistants Cecilia Baduria-Unger, Lydia Ramos and Aberash Zewde, who enabled me to complete it in this same spirit. To Nikolay Bolshakov, Information Officer, I owe tremendous thanks for his commitment to the idea of this unorthodox documentation, and his patient supervision and participation during its realization. Susanna Johnston, Chief of UN Publications, and Mark Holburn, of Jonathan Cape Ltd, also made highly appreciated efforts on behalf of this work, as did Bonnie Levinson at the New York Public Library.

I wish to give special thanks to Dr Colin McCabe of the British Film Institute for enabling the collaboration between myself and Christopher Hitchens.

To my friends who have been instrumental with help and inspiration over the course of this project, I am deeply and happily indebted.